How To Live
Worry-Free

How to Live

HOW TO LIVE WORRY-FREE

Kenneth Hagin Jr.

Unless otherwise indicated, all Scripture quotations in this volume are from the *King James Version* of the Bible.

First Printing 1996

ISBN 0-89276-735-9

In the U.S. write:
Kenneth Hagin Ministries
P.O. Box 50126
Tulsa, OK 74150-0126

In Canada write:
Kenneth Hagin Ministries
P.O. Box 335, Station D,
Etobicoke (Toronto), Ontario
Canada, M9A 4X3

BOOKS BY KENNETH E. HAGIN

* Redeemed From Poverty, Sickness and Spiritual Death
* What Faith Is
* Seven Vital Steps To Receiving the Holy Spirit
* Right and Wrong Thinking
  Prayer Secrets
* Authority of the Believer (foreign only)
* How To Turn Your Faith Loose
  The Key to Scriptural Healing
  Praying To Get Results
  The Present-Day Ministry of Jesus Christ
  The Gift of Prophecy
  Healing Belongs to Us
  The Real Faith
  How You Can Know the Will of God
  The Threefold Nature of Man
  The Human Spirit
  Turning Hopeless Situations Around
  Casting Your Cares Upon the Lord
  Seven Steps for Judging Prophecy
* The Interceding Christian
  Faith Food for Autumn
* Faith Food for Winter
  Faith Food for Spring
  Faith Food for Summer
* New Thresholds of Faith
* Prevailing Prayer to Peace
* Concerning Spiritual Gifts
  Bible Faith Study Course
  Bible Prayer Study Course
  The Holy Spirit and His Gifts
* The Ministry Gifts (Study Guide)
  Seven Things You Should Know About Divine Healing
  El Shaddai
  Zoe: The God-Kind of Life
  A Commonsense Guide to Fasting
  Must Christians Suffer?
  The Woman Question
  The Believer's Authority
  Ministering to Your Family
  What To Do When Faith Seems Weak and Victory Lost
  Growing Up, Spiritually
  Bodily Healing and the Atonement (Dr. T.J. McCrossan)
  Exceedingly Growing Faith
  Understanding the Anointing
  I Believe in Visions
  Understanding How To Fight the Good Fight of Faith
  Plans, Purposes, and Pursuits
  How You Can Be Led by the Spirit of God
  A Fresh Anointing
  Classic Sermons
  He Gave Gifts Unto Men:
      A Biblical Perspective of Apostles, Prophets, and Pastors
  The Art of Prayer
  Following God's Plan For Your Life

The Triumphant Church: Dominion Over All the Powers of Darkness
Healing Scriptures
Mountain-Moving Faith
Love: The Way to Victory
Biblical Keys to Financial Prosperity
Jesus — The Open Door
The Price Is Not Greater Than God's Grace (Mrs. Oretha Hagin)

MINIBOOKS (A partial listing)

* *The New Birth*
* *Why Tongues?*
* *In Him*
* *God's Medicine*
* *You Can Have What You Say*
* *Don't Blame God*
* *How To Keep Your Healing*
  The Bible Way To Receive the Holy Spirit
  I Went to Hell
  How To Walk in Love
  The Precious Blood of Jesus
* *Love Never Fails*
  How God Taught Me About Prosperity

BOOKS BY KENNETH HAGIN JR.

* *Man's Impossibility — God's Possibility*
  Because of Jesus
  How To Make the Dream God Gave You Come True
  The Life of Obedience
  Forget Not!
  God's Irresistible Word
  Healing: Forever Settled
  Don't Quit! Your Faith Will See You Through
  The Untapped Power in Praise
  Listen to Your Heart
  What Comes After Faith?
  Speak to Your Mountain!
  Come Out of the Valley!
  It's Your Move!
  God's Victory Plan
  Another Look at Faith
  How To Live Worry-Free
  Soaring With the Eagles

MINIBOOKS (A partial listing)

* *Faith Worketh by Love*
* *Seven Hindrances to Healing*
* *The Past Tense of God's Word*
  Faith Takes Back What the Devil's Stolen
  How To Be a Success in Life
  Unforgiveness
  Ministering to the Brokenhearted

*These titles are also available in Spanish. Information about other foreign translations of several of the above titles (i.e., Finnish, French, German, Indonesian, Polish, Russian, etc.) may be obtained by writing to: Kenneth Hagin Ministries, P.O. Box 50126, Tulsa, Oklahoma 74150-0126.

Contents

Why Be Worry-Free? Because God Cares About You. . . . 1

The Destructive Power of Worry 17

Conquer Worry By Conquering Your Thoughts! 25

You Have Authority Over Worry! 41

Chapter 1
Why Be Worry-Free?
Because God Cares About You!

Have you ever heard someone say, "Nobody cares about me"? Or maybe you have felt at times that there was no one around who really cared. You might be feeling right now that nobody cares about you. But I tell you, there is Someone who cares infinitely more than you can realize or understand. *God* cares about you!

1 PETER 5:7
7 Casting all your care upon him; for he careth for you.

1 PETER 5:7 (*NIV*)
7 Cast all your anxiety on him because he cares for you.

Care and anxiety carry with them the connotation of *fear*, *worry*, or *concern*. But you can cast your cares, anxieties, fears, worries, and concerns over on God — because He cares! Then you can get up and move on with God, free of those cares, and make something out of your life spiritually and naturally!

Throw Off the Burden of Your Cares!

What does it mean to cast your cares over on the Lord? Well, to "cast" means to *throw off, throw aside,* or *throw away.* We are not to go through life burdened down with cares. We can throw off and cast aside all of our cares, for God cares for us!

The *Moffatt's* translation of First Peter 5:7 says, "Let all your anxieties fall upon him. . . ."

The *Williams* translation says, "Cast every worry you have upon Him. . . ."

The *Knox* translation says, "Throw back on him the burden of all your anxiety. . . ."

The *Amplified* version says, "Casting the whole of your care [all your anxieties, all your worries, all your concerns, once and for all] on Him. . . ."

Many people take a stab at casting their cares on the Lord. They will give it a try, but the Bible doesn't say to give it a try. The Bible says we're to *do* it — we're to cast our cares *once and for all* on Him.

In my own life and ministry, I have to put First Peter 5:7 into practice on a regular basis. Being the executive director of Kenneth Hagin Ministries is an awesome responsibility in itself. But in addition to that, I also pastor a local church of about seven thousand members.

Then, too, I have the responsibility of helping run RHEMA Bible Training Center, where I also teach several classes. Besides that, we have two affiliate training centers internationally. We also print about five million books and distribute thousands of teaching tapes each year.

That's only a part of what this ministry does. And do you know what it takes to keep everything going? It takes something called *money*!

There are times I begin to feel the care, the load, and the pressure of the everyday operation of the ministry. I feel the weight of the responsibility that I have to make sure everything runs smoothly and in order.

But when I'm tempted to buckle under the load, I say, "No! This is God's ministry. If He can't make it go, I sure can't! I'm just the overseer. I'm going to do everything I know to do. I'm going to do everything I can with the knowledge and ability I have. But I am not going to worry!"

That's what some of you need to do with your own life. You need to make up your mind you're not going to worry, because God cares for you!

Now look particularly at the last part of First Peter 5:7: *". . . he careth for you."*

The *Twentieth Century New Testament* translation says, ". . . he makes you his care." That means when you cast your cares over on Him, He makes you His number-one priority!

Beck's translation says, ". . . He takes care of you."

The *Phillip's* translation says, ". . . you are his personal concern."

We need to understand that God is omnipresent. In other words, He is present in all places at all times. And God is personally concerned about and will be personally involved in the life of everyone who will come to Him and give Him his cares and burdens.

Now God will not come into your life and override your will. He will not come into your life and make you do something you don't want to do. No, you have to take the first step by going to Him with your cares.

Why do we have to take the first step? Because, really, He made the first step when He gave us His Son Jesus! Then He told us in His Word what belongs to us in Christ. Now it's up to us to do something about it. He cares!

Other translations of First Peter 5:7 read: ". . . his great interest is in you"; ". . . you are his charge"; ". . . he is concerned for you"; ". . . He cares for you affectionately, and cares about you watchfully." I think you can readily see that God cares for you!

God Demonstrated His Care for Us

Do you believe that God really cares about you? He cared enough about all of us to send us the Savior, Jesus Christ.

> **JOHN 3:16**
> **16 For God so loved the world, that he gave his only begotten Son, that whosoever believeth in him should not perish, but have everlasting life.**

God cared enough for mankind to redeem each and every one of us. Think about it for a moment. Do you realize that when man messed up and sinned in the Garden of Eden, God could have said, "All right, you've separated yourself from Me. You've done your own thing, and you've messed up. Now you stay where you are, eternally separated from Me. I'm going to create some new people to glorify Me."

God could have done that! But He didn't. Why? Because He cares for us!

Somebody said, "Well, I don't know if He could have abandoned man or not."

To answer that question, all you have to do is read the account in the Old Testament where God delivered the children of Israel out of Egypt to take them to the Promised Land. The children of Israel kept messing up until, finally, God told Moses, "I'm going to do away with this bunch. I'm tired of putting up with them" (Num. 14:11,12). But Moses talked God out of destroying the people (vv. 13-20).

You see, God didn't abandon Adam and Eve in the Garden, because He cared about them! Then He cared enough about all of us to send Jesus to redeem mankind.

And then after God sent His Son, He still cared enough about us to send us the Holy Spirit.

ACTS 2:4
4 And they were all filled with the Holy Ghost, and began to speak with other tongues, as the Spirit gave them utterance.

God sent us the Holy Spirit to help us overcome all of our tests, trials, and tribulations. The Holy Spirit is here to deliver us and teach us. We have the power of the Spirit available to us because God cares!

God also cared enough about us to provide healing for us. Jesus took stripes upon His back for our healing. First Peter 2:24 says, ". . . *by whose stripes ye were healed.*"

God cares for us!

The Sustaining Power of God

God cares about us and will sustain us by His power in the midst of any situation or circumstance we may face in life.

> **PSALM 55:22**
> **22 Cast thy burden upon the Lord, and he shall sustain thee: he shall never suffer the righteous to be moved.**

Cast your cares on the Lord, and He will do what? He will sustain you! That means He will *keep you*; He will *take care of you*. He cares!

I want you to notice that there's an implication in Psalm 55:22 that if we *don't* cast our cares or burdens on the Lord, He *won't* take care of us. It only says that He will take care of us *after* we've given Him our burdens.

Therefore, we don't have to wonder any longer why things sometimes don't go right in our lives. It's because we are carrying our cares! We are trying to handle the situation ourselves and trying to make something happen on our own. But if we could have done anything about most of the problems we face in life, we would have already done it!

Often, there's nothing we can do in the natural about a particular situation or circumstance. But God can! And all He asks us to do is to cast our cares on Him.

So make the decision to quit worrying about whatever it is you may be going through. You hold up your end of the bargain, so to speak, by casting your burdens on Him, and let God hold up *His* end of the bargain. We are to do the casting, and He is to do the sustaining!

God Cares Enough To Supply All of Our Needs

Not only did God care enough about us to provide us with salvation, the gift of the Holy Spirit, and healing for our bodies, He cares enough about us to meet our personal needs.

PHILIPPIANS 4:19
19 But my God shall supply all your need according to his riches in glory by Christ Jesus.

God *will* supply all of our needs if we will let Him. But once we believe and trust Him, we can't just sit down and do nothing and still expect Philippians 4:19 to work for us. For example, the Word also says, "Pay your tithes" (Mal. 3:10). Then after our tithes, the Bible says we are to give offerings.

Many times people can't give big offerings beyond their tithes at first. But the tithe is the ten percent of their increase that they owe, so they pay tithes first. Then later, they are able to give bigger offerings.

I always tell my church congregation to give something beyond their tithes in every offering, even if it's just a penny or a nickel. The amount is not important. I encourage them not to let an offering bucket go by that they don't put something in. Then I tell them to believe that God will multiply their seed and give back to them so they'll prosper more and be able to give more.

God is faithful to His Word. If He says, "You do this, and I'll bless you," then if you do what He told you to do, you *will* be blessed!

Let's look again at what God told us to do in Malachi 3:10. He says, *"Bring ye all the tithes into the storehouse, that there may be meat in mine house, and PROVE ME NOW HEREWITH, saith the Lord of hosts, if I will not OPEN YOU THE WINDOWS OF HEAVEN, and POUR YOU OUT A BLESSING, that THERE SHALL NOT BE ROOM ENOUGH TO RECEIVE IT."*

Now look at verse 11: *"And I will rebuke the devourer for your sakes, and he shall not destroy the fruits of your ground; neither shall your vine cast her fruit before the time in the field, saith the Lord of hosts."*

Some people say, "I can't afford to pay my tithes."

You can't afford *not* to!

When I was an associate pastor years ago, a young man came to me and said, "I get paid on Friday and cash my check on the way home from work. Before Sunday gets here, I've already spent almost everything I made that week, so I don't always pay my tithes."

The young man continued, "I have been tracking it for the last six months or so, and I've discovered that every week I don't pay tithes, something happens to my car, my house, or to something else that takes the exact amount I would have tithed to repair it."

I told him, "All right, I'll tell you what you can do. I'm going to give you some tithing envelopes. When you cash your paycheck, put the tithe money in the envelope right then. And if you don't trust yourself not to touch it before Sunday, preaddress each envelope. Then when you get paid, put your tithe in the envelope, put a stamp on it, and drop it in the mailbox on your way home."

This young man and his family were barely getting along before we had that conversation. But he started doing what I told him to do, and pretty soon, he got a better job, and all kinds of good things began to happen in their lives. They were getting blessed coming and going!

That young man told me later, "I'm not worried or concerned about finances anymore. God is blessing us just as He said He would, and I trust Him to continue to meet our needs."

You see, before that, this man was always concerned about money and the welfare of his family, because the money just wasn't there to meet the need. But when he began to obey God and do what He said to do, he got blessed!

You can be blessed, too, because God is no respecter of persons (Acts 10:34). What He does for one person who obeys Him, He will do for anyone else who obeys Him. So do what God told you to do in His Word and expect to be blessed!

Perseverance Pays Off!

But you can't obey God haphazardly or sporadically. You have to *consistently* obey God to receive the blessings.

You see, patience and perseverance are the keys to receiving the blessings of God. Have you ever started out obeying God, but then your situation didn't look like it was improving? You obeyed, but it didn't look like you were making any gain or headway.

In the natural, when some people try to lose weight, at first it can look as if nothing is happening even though they are eating and exercising properly. But if these people will keep doing what they've been doing — eating right and exercising — after a few months, seemingly all of a sudden, they will notice a difference! They may not see the desired result all at once, but if they keep up their good eating habits and their exercise program over a period of time, they will see more and more results.

That's the way it is with believing God. You may not see an instant change in your circumstances, but if you will keep doing God's Word, it *will* pay off! You will see results!

God's paydays are not every Friday or Saturday. Sometimes God's paydays are not every week, every month, or even every six months. But if you keep doing what God tells you to do, payday will come! God cares about you! He cares enough to make things happen for you when you believe and trust Him. Your responsibility is to keep trusting, believing, and casting your cares on Him.

You see, faith has a part to play in casting our cares on the Lord. It takes faith to let go of our problems and give them to God, believing He will take care of them. Then after we give our problems to God, we are to go on our way, carefree and worry-free. That's faith!

We need to understand that everything we do in walking with God, serving Him, and doing what He said to do involves faith. Faith is the foundation of our Christian walk. The Bible says, "The just shall live by faith" (Rom. 1:17; Gal. 3:11; Heb. 10:38).

We can't do anything to please God without faith (Heb. 11:6). But God is pleased when we consistently trust and obey Him and give Him all of our worries and cares. He cares about us, so we don't have to be concerned about the tests and trials of life. We don't have to be burdened down and consumed with worry and fear. We can live our lives worry-free!

Learn To Rest in the Lord

What does it mean to be worry-free? If you are worry-free, it means you are resting in the Lord and His Word. It means you are totally committed to believing and trusting Him, and you have His peace.

This passage in Psalm 37 shows you how to rest in the Lord and let *Him* take care of your problems and cares.

PSALM 37:5-7
5 COMMIT THY WAY UNTO THE LORD; TRUST ALSO IN HIM; and HE shall bring it to pass.

6 And he shall bring forth thy righteousness as the light, and thy judgment as the noonday.
7 Rest in the Lord, and wait patiently for him: FRET NOT THYSELF because of him who prospereth in his way, because of the man who bringeth wicked devices [schemes] to pass.

Some people may *start out* believing and trusting God for something. But then they see the wicked getting blessed and begin to say, "Well, I might as well be over there with the sinners, doing what they're doing. It seems they're getting blessed more than I'm getting blessed."

But, no. You stay true to God, and He'll stay true to you! But if you depart from His Word, He won't have anything to work with in your life. God works in line with His Word, so unless you trust Him and commit your way to Him, He can't help you like He wants to, because He can't go against His Word.

Psalm 37:8 says, *"Cease from anger, and forsake wrath: fret not thyself in any wise to do evil."* One translation says, "Refrain from anger, and forsake wrath. . . ."

Fretting is the same as worrying. If you allow yourself to become overly wrought up or anxious about something, you will begin fretting.

God will take care of you in life if you trust Him. He will sustain and see you through any difficulty. But you can't be fretful or worrisome and at the same time say you're trusting God.

Look at verse 7 of Psalm 37 again: *"REST IN THE LORD, and wait patiently for him: fret not thyself because of him who prospereth in his way, because of the man who bringeth wicked devices to pass."* God wants us to learn to rest in Him.

What are some of the results of *not* resting in the Lord? If you're not resting in the Lord, you're worrying. You're fretting and becoming anxious. If you're not casting all of your cares on the Lord and resting in Him, you will lose sleep. You'll become a bundle of nerves, so to speak. You could become an accident going somewhere to "explode"! That's why it's so important to learn to rest in the Lord.

Many times in the Word of God you can find the words "rest in the Lord" or a variation of that same message, such as "Be not afraid." When you're at rest, you're not afraid. You're not worried or concerned.

I didn't say you weren't concerned from the standpoint of being slothful and apathetic with an "I-don't-care" attitude. But you aren't concerned in the sense you're fretting and having anxiety either. Why? Because you've cast your cares over on the Lord and you're resting and trusting in Him.

Cast Your Cares Once and for All

If you want to live in the fullness of your salvation, you must learn to cast your cares, fears, anxieties, worries, and concerns over on the Lord once and for all.

Get hold of the fact that your abundant living depends upon whether or not you cast all of your cares on the Lord. As you cast all your burdens on Him, He will take care of you. Do you believe that?

If you do believe it, then you need to go ahead and cast your cares on the Lord!

Now God won't come and just "rip" your cares away from you. Remember I said He won't do anything against your will — without your cooperation.

No, you have to gather your cares up yourself and say, "All right, Lord, here are my problems. I'm doing what You told me to do; I'm casting all my cares on You. Now You take care of them." Whether it be problems with money, your health, your children, your job, or *any* problem, God cares, and you can cast your cares on Him.

So it's not up to God to come and get your burdens. It's up to you to go to Him with them and to once and for all leave them there!

When I was in the U.S. Army, during a drill our squadron had to march out to a certain destination in full gear, with our field packs and weapons. Then we had to march all the way back, still loaded down with all that heavy equipment.

We marched to the specified location, and the colonel who supervised the training regiment said, "You guys beat everybody in the entire regiment!" The company that was closest to us at the time was three minutes behind us.

As we started to march back to our starting point, the lieutenant stopped us near a truck that was parked beside the road. He said, "Take off all your packs and throw them in the truck. We're going to march back without them."

Do you know what happened? There was not one person in that squadron who said, "Oh, no, that's all right. Thank you anyway, but I'll carry my own pack." No! We all ran over to that truck and dumped those packs in a hurry! It felt so good to get rid of that heavy gear!

But many times when it comes to casting our cares or burdens on the Lord, Christians will tell God, "No, thank You, God. I'll just carry this burden myself."

Then some people will cast their care on the Lord, saying, "Here it is, Lord. Here is my care." Then when they finish praying, they grab hold of that burden and take it right back. But the Bible says they are to take their cares to God and *leave* them there!

When our lieutenant told us to throw our packs into that truck, there wasn't one soldier running after that truck to try to get back his pack!

That's what we have to do spiritually — we have to cast our cares on the Lord and leave them there. Then we have to go on about our business, believing He will take care of them. We can't go back and pick up those cares ever again.

My Challenge to You

Your success in life spiritually and naturally depends on how much you trust the Lord and whether or not you cast your cares on Him. Your success depends on your obedience to God and His Word.

I challenge you to cast your cares on the Lord right now. I challenge you to move into new arenas of victorious

living with God by living a worry-free life that is pleas-
ing to Him. If you'll commit yourself to resting and
trusting in God, you will move up a notch spiritually. If
you need to ask God to forgive you for worrying, then do
it and receive your forgiveness. Then go on down the
road of life worry-free, because God cares for you!

Chapter 2
The Destructive Power
Of Worry

*Casting all your care upon him; for he careth
for you.*

— 1 Peter 5:7

*Cast thy burden upon the Lord, and he shall
sustain thee: he shall never suffer the righteous
to be moved.*

— Psalm 55:22

Do you believe that God is big enough to take care of
every aspect of your life — of everything that concerns
you? Your faith in God's willingness and ability to take
care of you will cause you to receive many blessings in
life as you trust yourself to His loving care. It will also
keep you from the sin of worry.

The Bible says that whatever is not of faith is sin
(Rom. 14:23). So to worry about anything instead of
trusting God to take care of the situation is a sin. *It is a
sin to worry!*

Worry Produces Nothing of Value

Not only is it a sin to worry, worry is *unproductive*. In other words, worrying doesn't change the circumstances you may face in life. Worrying only keeps you from looking to God and getting your answer.

Let's look at Matthew chapter 6 to see what worrying accomplishes.

> **MATTHEW 6:25-30**
> **25 Therefore I say unto you, Take no thought for your life, what ye shall eat, or what ye shall drink; nor yet for your body, what ye shall put on. Is not the life more than meat, and the body than raiment?**
> **26 Behold the fowls of the air: for they sow not, neither do they reap, nor gather into barns; yet your heavenly Father feedeth them. Are ye not much better than they?**
> **27 Which of you by TAKING THOUGHT [worrying] can add one cubit unto his stature?**
> **28 And why take ye thought for raiment? Consider the lilies of the field, how they grow; they toil not, neither do they spin:**
> **29 And yet I say unto you, That even Solomon in all his glory was not arrayed like one of these.**
> **30 Wherefore, if God so clothe the grass of the field, which to day is, and to morrow is cast into the oven, shall he not much more clothe you, O ye of LITTLE FAITH?**

Verse 30 implies that a person who is taking thought for his life or worrying is a person who has little faith.

Then verse 27 says, *"Which of you by TAKING THOUGHT can add one cubit unto his stature?"* In other words, worrying can't make you an inch shorter or an inch taller. So we see that worry is not only a sin, it accomplishes nothing productive or of any value.

A Small Problem With a Big Shadow

What does worry do? Worry makes a small problem look big. Or you could say it like this: *Worry gives a small problem a big shadow.*

By way of illustration, did you ever notice that if the rays of the sun hit an object just right, the object will cast a shadow? The object can just be something small, but at certain times of the day, it can cast a huge shadow!

That's what the devil likes to do with situations and circumstances in our lives. He likes to magnify even the small problems in our lives that we may be tempted to worry about. He tries to make us worry when those things are not to be worried about!

You may be facing many frustrating situations in your life. You may even be looking at some circumstances that look impossible. But I want you to understand that you cannot surprise God with whatever you take to Him, big or small. He already knows about it! And to Him, that situation is just a small problem with a big shadow!

Our text says, "Casting the whole of your care [all your anxieties, all your worries, all your concerns, once and for all] on Him . . ." (*Amp.*).

The *New International Version* of that verse says, "Cast all your *anxiety. . . .*"

Now the *King James Version* simply says, *"Casting all your CARE upon him; for he careth for you."* But we have already seen in chapter 1 that these two words "care" and "anxiety" include *worry, fear,* and *concern.*

So then you could say without doing harm to the Scripture, "Casting all your care, anxiety, worry, and concern on Him, because He cares for you."

The Lord wants us to walk worry-free! He wants us to walk in joy and in peace! He wants us to walk in liberty and to enjoy life.

But if you're all tied up and bound with care and worry, you are not at peace. You are not at liberty, and you are not free to enjoy life!

Have you ever been bound with worry? If you have, you know that worry causes you not to enjoy life to the fullest. No matter where you are or what you're doing, that worry is always gnawing at you.

Worry takes the joy out of living. But God wants you to be free from worry. He wants you to live worry-free!

The Mark of a Person Who's Living Worry-Free

How can you tell if a person is living free from worry? The mark of a child of God who is worry-free is the joy and peace he exhibits *even in the midst of persecution and affliction.* The person who is worry-free lives like a person with no problems *in spite of* his unpleasant circumstances. I didn't say he never has any problems. I said he is carefree because he trusts in the Lord!

Why can a person live carefree even in the midst of tests and trials? Because he knows that God is going to take care of him and his situation. He believes that what God's Word says is true. And when a person believes that and casts his care on the Lord, he can rest secure and worry-free.

If *you* want to be a person who's worry-free, you need to declare from your heart, "I am what the Word says I am. I can do what the Word says I can do. And I can have what the Word says I can have."

You must learn to act on the Word if you want to live worry-free and enjoy a rich, full life in God. It doesn't matter what's happening around you — if the thunder is rolling, the lightning is flashing, and the storms of life are assailing — if you learn to cast or roll your care on the Lord according to the Word, you *can* be worry-free.

That's exciting news! Most people want to live an abundant worry-free life in God. I don't know of too many who want to be robbed of the blessings of God through worry! The Bible says, *"The thief cometh not, but for TO STEAL, and TO KILL, and TO DESTROY: I am come that they might have life, and that they might have it more ABUNDANTLY"* (John 10:10).

Worry is a thief and a robber. Worry robs you of your joy, your peace, and the blessings God wants you to have. But you can make the decision never to let worry steal from you again, as you do what the Word says to do and cast your cares on the Lord!

Fear Follows Worry

What exactly is worry? For one thing, worry is *fear triumphing over faith.* In other words, where there is worry, there cannot be faith. But on the other hand, where there is faith, there cannot be worry. So if you are worrying about something, your worry is triumphing over your faith. But if you're exercising faith, your faith is triumphing over worry!

It's been said that worry is fear's right hand. Did you ever notice that the minute you begin to succumb to worry, you begin to be fearful too? But the Bible says, *"For God hath not given us the spirit of fear; but of power, and of love, and of a sound mind"* (2 Tim. 1:7).

Worry causes you to be afraid of something. Do you remember I said that worry makes a small problem seem big? Fear is much the same way. Many times the devil magnifies something in your mind, and if you give place to those thoughts, you become more and more afraid. Most of the time, you're worried and afraid about something that doesn't even exist or that hasn't even materialized.

By way of illustration, I remember when I was a little boy, there were times I'd become afraid in the nighttime. I slept in a room in the back of the house that was separate from the rest of the family. Until I was in the eighth grade, I slept on a roll-away bed that I put wherever I could find room. When the weather was warmer, I slept on our screened-in back porch.

And do you know what? If there was a shadow from the moonlight, a streetlight that seemed to move behind the window shade, or if I heard some unusual noise, I'd become afraid.

Then when I was a little older, one night I heard something outside, and I saw a shadow outside my window. So I got up to go see what it was. I thought to myself, *I'm tired of this! Why have I been lying here feeling afraid? I don't even know what it is I'm afraid of.*

So I opened the back door and went outside to investigate. As it turned out, the shadow I saw and the noise I heard was nothing more than a big tree limb scraping the roof! A streetlight was causing the tree limb to cast a shadow that looked like somebody's arm moving across the window!

There I'd been, afraid of a tree limb scraping the roof of the house! I'd been lying in bed afraid that any minute somebody was going to come through that window and get me!

I'm sure many of you have had similar experiences. You can identify with my experience, and you've probably done the same thing I did! You see, I was worried and afraid over nothing! The situation looked like something it was not, and I was concerned about something that didn't even exist!

That's exactly what the devil tries to get people to do — to get them to worry and become fearful about things that don't amount to anything. When he can get them worrying, he can steal from them. He can rob them of happiness and joy. Satan can destroy a person's life through worry.

But we do not have to be robbed! We can live worry-free if we'll just do what God says to do. God doesn't want us burdened down with cares. He has made provision for us to cast our worries and cares on Him.

The Consequences of Worry

Did you know that worry and anxiety will affect you in every area of your life? It will hinder you on your job, because you can't work efficiently when you have your mind on a problem or care. When you worry, your productivity and efficiency are very much hampered.

Physicians tell us that if a person continues to live with anxiety and care, it could result in heart problems, blood pressure problems, and mental problems. In fact, some physicians tell us that worry can lead to paranoia, which is a form of fear. As I said, fear follows worry. Worry and anxiety will bring fear into your life.

Also, have you ever noticed that a person who is burdened down with cares and anxieties always looks sad. He sort of hangs his head in defeat; he doesn't have any joy.

But a person who has learned to cast his burden on the Lord walks around with a smile on his face and with his head held high! This person knows that even though problems and fear and worry come, he can turn them over to the Lord and let the Lord handle them. This person has learned the secret of living worry-free!

Don't let worry rob you and destroy your life. You don't have to be defeated by worry, because you can cast your worries on the Lord. You *can* live life worry-free!

Chapter 3
Conquer Worry
By Conquering Your
Thoughts!

We know that worry is fear triumphing over faith. Worry is also *the misuse of the imagination God has placed within us.*

Have you ever just sat quietly, thinking and meditating on the Word of God? Did you realize that as you were meditating, you were using your creative imagination?

God gave man the ability to imagine. He gave us our creative imagination. We are to use our imaginations properly, according to the Word of God, so we can envision our lives the way they are supposed to be — the way God intends our lives to be.

But without renewing our minds with the Word, we'll use our imaginations improperly. We'll only see our circumstances the way they appear, and we'll live powerless to change those circumstances.

Seeing With the Eye of Faith

I made the statement one time that as a person meditates in line with the Word of God, he sees things as they *really are* according to God's Word, not just the way they *appear* in the natural. You see, one way you view your circumstances is with the eye of *faith*; the other way you view your circumstances is with your physical eyes.

People sometimes define the circumstances they see as *reality*. But we who see with the eye of faith have a higher truth to trust in — the Word of God.

When you use your imagination properly or in line with God's Word, you can begin to see things with the eye of faith. The circumstances in the natural may be unpleasant, but you are imagining or seeing the answer according to the Word. Some people call it daydreaming with the Holy Ghost! Others simply call it meditating on the Word.

For example, if you are facing financial trouble or lack, with the eye of faith you can begin to see yourself prosperous and having plenty. Why? Because when you're thinking and meditating in line with the Word and you're trusting God, even if your pockets are empty, you can begin to see yourself with a pocketful! In other words, you are believing God to take care of the situation and that He will meet your need.

Or if you're facing sickness or disease, with the eye of faith you can begin to see yourself well, whole, and healthy. You see yourself according to the Word (1 Peter 2:24). This is how to properly use your God-given creative imagination — in line with His Word.

Train Your Thoughts To Work
For You, Not *Against* You

How does worry begin? It begins with a thought or an imagination. When you dwell on the wrong thing, it gives you a negative feeling and worry begins to set in.

Often that happens because we are analyzing a certain situation instead of going to the Word for our answers and taking the situation to God.

Have you ever heard the expressions "paralysis by analysis" or "too much analyzing leads to paralysis"? When you analyze a situation instead of simply going to God with it and trusting Him, you can become paralyzed, feeling helpless and confused.

When situations confront you, don't use your own natural reasoning to analyze them and forget the Word. You can find your answer in the Word!

In a test or trial, instead of praying and committing the problem to God, some people will say, "Oh, why did this happen to me?" They become so involved in trying to figure out why something happened that they actually forget to pray and trust God for the answer! They begin worrying instead of praying and believing God.

Really, in the midst of a test or trial, it shouldn't be a matter of asking "Why did God let this happen?" It should be more a matter of just trusting Him and doing what He said to do in His Word. The Bible says, *"Trust in the Lord with all thine heart; and lean not unto thine own understanding"* (Prov. 3:5). That's how the victory comes — through trust and faith, not through worrying, fretting, and having anxiety.

Remember I said that worry never accomplishes anything productive. Worry never produces victory because worry is fear triumphing over faith. Worry is the misuse of the creative imagination God has given you. Worry will rob you of God's promises. Worry is *the highway that leads from somewhere to nowhere!* So don't travel on the highway of worry. Stay off that road!

After you've made the decision to trust God and not worry, the devil will still put thoughts in your mind to try to make you worry and fret. But you have to resist those thoughts. You have to go back to thinking in line with the Word and seeing yourself blessed.

Casting Down Vain Imaginations

Somebody may say, "Wait a minute! The Bible says, *'CASTING DOWN imaginations, and every high thing that exalteth itself against the knowledge of God, and bringing into captivity every thought to the obedience of Christ'* [2 Cor. 10:5]. And you're telling me to *imagine* something?"

But let's look at that scripture in its setting.

2 CORINTHIANS 10:4,5
4 (For the weapons of our warfare are not carnal, but mighty through God to the pulling down of strong holds;)
5 Casting down imaginations, and every high thing that exalteth itself against the knowledge of God, and bringing into captivity every thought to the obedience of Christ.

Notice that verse 5 says, *"Casting down imagina-tions, and every high thing THAT EXALTETH ITSELF AGAINST THE KNOWLEDGE OF GOD. . . ."* In other words, you're to cast down imaginations that tell you God's Word isn't true and you're not going to make it in life. You're to cast down the thoughts that say you can't receive your healing and be made whole.

Those thoughts are contrary to the knowledge of God, because the Word plainly says we can be healed, walk in health, and experience abundant victory in life. So it's the vain imaginations *that exalt themselves against the knowledge* of God that we are to cast down and not think about!

The Bible never said, "Don't imagine." It simply said, "Cast down imaginations that exalt themselves against the knowledge of God."

You see, the "knowledge of God" says, "You're healed" (Isa. 53:5). So you have every right to imagine and see yourself healed. You have every right to believe God for healing, because when you believe for healing, your believing is based on the authority of God's Word.

The Word of God or the knowledge of God also says, *"But my God shall supply all your need according to his riches in glory by Christ Jesus"* (Phil. 4:19). So, you see, you have the authority to imagine yourself prosperous and with all your needs met.

Because God promised in His Word to meet your needs, you can begin to imagine what you're going to do when the money comes in that you were believing God for! You can begin to see yourself giving more money to missions. You can begin to see yourself in a new suit or dress. You can see yourself with a better car. You can begin to see yourself buying a new house. You can see yourself with the new tires you need for the car you have. Why? Because of God's Word, you can see yourself with *all* your needs supplied!

We receive those things we need, because we have committed everything to God and His plan, and He is in control. We trust and believe Him to meet all our needs, and we see it as done!

Imagination that is operating in line with God's Word is like the blueprint for whatever it is you're believing for. For example, as the Pastor, I could envision and imagine our church auditorium when there was nothing on the piece of land where the church now sits but the dirt and grass!

Then as the steel was being put up and the walls were erected around the structural work, there was still nothing there but a shell that resembled a building. But I saw in my mind's eye our church auditorium!

I would bring my pastoral staff to the construction site and show them where the pulpit would be. I'd show them where the choir loft and orchestra pit were going to be. I'd describe to them the arrangement of all the pews and where the front of the altar would be where we'd have prayer lines and pray for the sick.

I saw it! I was properly using the imagination God gave me, because what I envisioned was in line with the knowledge of God's plan for our church.

We should give place to God's purposes and plans for us as we meditate and believe God's Word. Those are the kinds of thoughts we are to give place to.

The kinds of thoughts we are *not* to give place to — the imaginations we are to cast down — are thoughts such as, *Oh, what am I going to do now? There's no way I can make it through this problem.* Those thoughts are vain imaginations of worry and fear that need to be cast down and brought under subjection to the obedience of Christ (2 Cor. 10:5).

Christ has said, "I have redeemed you from the curse of the Law. I was made a curse for you that the blessing of Abraham might come on the Gentiles through Me" (Gal. 3:13,14). Now my mind can work with *that*! I can easily meditate and think upon that kind of thought! *I am redeemed!* The Word of God says I am! But I cannot afford to allow myself to think upon any thoughts that are not in line with God's Word.

Don't Be Ignorant of Satan's Devices

Some people don't have a problem with worry in and of itself. But one trick of the enemy is to get people off track with the Word in one area of their lives so he can snare them in another area.

For example, some people don't have a problem with worry, but they are weak in the area of forgiving others. The devil will try to trip those people up with unforgiveness. Then once he has them dwelling on unforgiving thoughts — thoughts that are contrary to the Word —

those same people will begin to have trouble thinking God's thoughts in other areas of their lives, such as healing. Then before they realize what's happening, they succumb to all kinds of thoughts, such as thoughts of worry, fear, doubt, unbelief, and so forth.

You just can't afford to think and act apart from God's Word! You have to cast down thoughts that exalt themselves against the knowledge of God no matter what another person may have done to hurt you. If someone has wronged you, and you see that person coming down the street, you need to walk right up to him and say, "Hello. How are you? God bless you." Don't ignore him.

A certain person wronged me once, and later I saw this person at a ball game. In fact, the person sat down behind me at the game. In my flesh, I wanted to turn around and really let him know what I thought about what he'd done!

I'm just telling you how I felt. I believe preachers need to be honest with others about these things. Some preachers just act pious, with a "holier-than-thou" attitude. But preachers are human too. They have some of the same thoughts and feelings that others have.

So what did I do when I realized this person was sitting behind me? I turned around, smiled, and said, "Hello, how are you doing? It's good to see you." I turned around again about ten minutes later, and he was gone! (Sometimes when you walk in the God-kind of love with those who've wronged you, they become agitated. They can't stand it! They want you to get in a verbal battle with them. But that's the world's way; that's not God's way.)

Walking in love and forgiveness starts with your thoughts. You've got to think good thoughts. Now I realize that some people aren't very nice, and they do wrong; they're not living right. But I'm going to give them the benefit of the doubt, so to speak. I'm not the Judge; God is. So, I'll just let Him judge, and I'm going to walk in love.

Somebody said, "Well, I just don't understand how So-and-so can say he is a Christian and still act the way he does."

I don't let situations like that bother me. I'm going to walk in love and just let God take care of those people.

God is the Judge, not us. In fact, God said in His Word that we would get into trouble if we tried to be the judge. So we have to cast down critical, judgmental thoughts, because if we're not careful, we can slip up and miss it in this area.

Somebody once said to me, "I don't think So-and-so ought to be up in church shouting, dancing, and praising the Lord. I don't believe he's living right."

I answered, "How do you know he's not living right? How do you know that since you last saw him, he hasn't repented and asked God to forgive him? The Bible says, *'If we confess our sins, he is faithful and just to forgive us our sins, and to cleanse us from all unrighteousness'"* (1 John 1:9).

According to First John 1:9, God is faithful to His Word to freely forgive us when we are truly sorry for our sin and ask for forgiveness. The Bible also says we are to forgive others (Matt. 18:21,22; Mark 11:25). And

Galatians 6:1 says, *"Brethren, if a man be overtaken in a fault, YE WHICH ARE SPIRITUAL, restore such an one in the spirit of meekness; considering thyself, lest thou also be tempted."* If we are spiritual, we will forgive and restore someone who has missed it; we won't judge him and criticize him.

So to live worry-free, you also have to live free of unforgiveness. And the decision to worry or not to worry or to forgive or not to forgive is affected by your thought-life.

Thinking and Living
In Line With God's Word

We've seen that there is nothing wrong with using our God-given creative imaginations to meditate on God's Word and see ourselves the way God sees us. It's only wrong when we don't use them in line with the Word of God. Second Corinthians 10:5 tells us so plainly in a nutshell what we aren't supposed to imagine: *"Casting down imaginations, and every high thing that exalteth itself against the knowledge of God, and bringing into captivity every thought to the obedience of Christ."* Therefore, we can know the thoughts we *are* supposed to dwell on and the thoughts we are *not* supposed to dwell on.

It's really very simple. We are only to think thoughts that are in line with the Word!

You see, the Gospel is simple; it's not complicated. Back in the days when Christ lived on the earth, He made serving God simple. It was the religious people who made it hard, because they made serving God nothing more than a bunch of man-made rules and regulations.

It's still the same way today, some two thousand years later. It hasn't changed. Man still has his tradition and his way of doing things.

For example, some religious people say, "If you don't come in line with our set of rules, you can't be saved."

Some of those people say, "If you don't get water-baptized, you're not really saved." But my response to a statement like that is, what happens to the person who from his heart asks for forgiveness and confesses Jesus as Lord five minutes before he dies? He will go to Heaven — that's what will happen to him! Jesus said, ". . . *him that cometh to me I will in no wise cast out*" (John 6:37)!

You see, we have to live our lives by what the Word says, not by what religion or tradition says that exalts itself against the knowledge of God's Word.

Another group says, "You have to take all your jewelry off before you can get filled with the Spirit."

I remember my dad telling the story of a certain woman who had come to the church altar to be filled with the Holy Spirit. Dad prayed with her as she knelt at the altar. She was filled with the Spirit and began speaking in tongues. Then as Dad went on to pray for someone else, he overheard a man talking to this woman. The man had walked up to where this woman was kneeling. He didn't know she'd already spoken in tongues. She was just praying quietly at the altar at that time.

The man said to the woman, "Sister, if you'll pull that wedding band off, God will fill you with the Spirit." Dad rushed over to the man and woman as quickly as he could and said, "Wait a minute, Brother. Hold it just a minute. God's *already* filled her with the Spirit — wedding band and all!"

You see, religion and man's tradition have their rules, but the Bible is the only true rule book for salvation and for the things of God. The Bible says, *"There is a way which seemeth right unto a man, but the end thereof are the ways of death"* (Prov. 14:12).

As I said, we are to live our lives by God's Word, not by man's ideas and traditions. And the Bible says that God's Word is full of power (Rom. 1:16)! We don't have to live as the world lives, because we have God's Word. We don't have to worry about the things the devil brings our way.

You have the ability and the authority to cast down worry and to resist anxious thoughts. You can use the same energy you've used in the past worrying and put that energy to better use by casting down vain imaginations and by casting your care over on the Lord.

Refuse To Be Robbed of the Word!

Some people spend all of their time and energy worrying about a particular situation instead of casting their cares over on the Lord and trusting Him to work it out. For instance, they'll say, "I just can't see any way out of this situation" or "I don't know how God is going to work this out. I don't know if everything will turn out all right or not." They lose sleep at night worrying about the problem. But when daylight comes, the problem is still there; nothing has changed.

When the devil tries to work on me with similar thoughts, I say, "All right, Mr. Devil. You want somebody to worry? Then *you* worry about it. But my Bible tells me *I* can cast my cares on the Lord, so I'm going to sleep in the Holy Ghost."

Sometimes I'll say, "I'm not going to worry about something I don't have any control over anyway. I know God has control of everything, and my faith is in Him." Then I quote the scriptures that cover whatever it is I need. I lay my head down on my pillow, praying in tongues, and I always fall fast asleep. Then I'm fresh the next day. I'm not tired and worn out physically, mentally, and emotionally from worrying, fretting, and having anxiety.

You see, the devil will try to keep you in an anxious state of mind, and he will eventually try to destroy your sanity. He will try to keep you fretful and worried so that you can't do anything right. As I said, worry is nothing but a thief and a robber.

Did you ever notice that most of the things a person worries about are things that never really happen? Still, the devil will come whisper in your ear, "What about this? What about that? What are you going to do?"

Dwelling on those thoughts is nothing more than wasted motion in the long run. Some of the enemy's threats are so far-fetched, you'd have to actually *try* to worry about them! Then if you do begin to worry, when you come to yourself, you say, "What in the world am I doing! Why am I worrying about *that!*"

When the devil comes to me with his "what ifs," I always have an answer from the Word. If he says, "What if such-and-such happens?" I'll say, "What about it? What if it *does* happen? God is still in control, and He's going to bring me out on top!"

The devil has no answer for that. He has no defense against the Word. He wants to get us thinking apart from the Word and dwelling on his negative thoughts so he can defeat us.

Did you ever notice that the devil's way of tripping you up is to ask you some question or put some question in your mind to get you to doubt God's Word? For example, all the way back in the Garden of Eden, the devil said to Eve, "Did God really say you mustn't eat of every tree in the garden?" (Gen. 3:1). Then after Eve told the serpent — the devil — what God had said, the devil came against God's Word. He came against the knowledge of God.

> **GENESIS 3:2-4**
> 2 And the woman said unto the serpent, We may eat of the fruit of the trees of the garden:
> 3 But of the fruit of the tree which is in the midst of the garden, God hath said, Ye shall not eat of it, neither shall ye touch it, lest ye die.
> 4 And the serpent said unto the woman, Ye shall not surely die.

You see, God said, ". . . *of the tree of the knowledge of good and evil, thou shalt not eat of it: for in the day that thou eatest thereof thou shalt surely die"* (Gen. 2:17). But the devil said to Eve, "You shall *not* die."

Then the devil added, *"For God doth know that in the day ye eat thereof, then your eyes shall be opened, and ye shall be as gods, knowing good and evil"* (Gen. 3:5).

The devil said in effect, "If you eat of that tree, you're going to be as smart as God is."

Now why did the devil say that? Because that's the way he operates. He takes just a part of the Word and twists it just enough to make it sound good. That's why it's important for us to *know* the Word, so we can cast down imaginations and every thing that exalts itself against the knowledge of God (2 Cor. 10:5).

The devil will come to us with questions, trying to get us offtrack so we'll begin thinking things that aren't in line with God's Word. That's how he gets us to worry. But the Bible says we are not to be ignorant of Satan's devices (2 Cor. 2:11). We can defeat the enemy at every turn in our lives if we know how he operates and stand fast against him with the truth of God's Word.

Set Your Heart and Mind on the Word

Worry is the enemy's tool to steal the Word of God from you and to make God's promises ineffective in your life. The devil uses worry to distract you from the Word and to get you to dwell on anxious, negative thoughts instead of on the Word. Then gradually, you are no longer thinking on the Word at all or trusting God to see you through to victory.

You see, you cannot worry *and* think on the Word at the same time. Likewise, you cannot think on the Word and worry at the same time! Therefore, we know what we are to think upon.

The Apostle Paul said, ". . . *whatsoever things are true, whatsoever things are honest, whatsoever things are just, whatsoever things are pure, whatsoever things are lovely, whatsoever things are of good report; if there be any virtue, and if there be any praise, think on THESE THINGS*" (Phil. 4:8)!

You can conquer worry in your life simply by conquering your thoughts and keeping your heart and mind set on God's Word!

Chapter 4
You Have Authority Over Worry!

One of the most important things you can realize is that Satan has no power over you unless you allow him to have it. You have authority over the devil and his bondage. Jesus said, *"Behold, I give unto you power to tread on serpents and scorpions, and over all the power of the enemy: and nothing shall by any means hurt you"* (Luke 10:19).

You see, most of the time, Christians play right into the devil's hands by waiting until they're being attacked before they begin to stand their ground on the Word and use their rightful authority in Christ. When they're faced with a certain situation or circumstance, they will become passive and apathetic. They will hesitate and only then try to arm themselves with enough Word to spiritually counter the immediate attack of the enemy.

But we don't have to be passive and hesitant! We need to become active concerning the things of God and get on the offensive in the sense of becoming assertive! We're the ones, not the devil, with power and authority from Heaven! We need to use that power and not allow any of the thoughts or tricks of the enemy to trip us up and cause us to be defeated by worry or by *anything* that's evil.

Now in the natural, there are times we need to learn how to be defensive. For example, there is such a thing as defensive driving. When you drive defensively, you anticipate the way another vehicle is going to move, and you prepare yourself or make your move accordingly. But even then, we need to be assertive in driving defensively. I tell you, there have been times I have used "aggressive driving" to avoid being caught in an accident!

For example, once I was driving down a particular expressway, and an accident involving several cars took place up ahead of me. Cars were spinning in every direction! Suddenly, I saw a gap between some cars, and in a split second, I made the decision to accelerate and shoot through the open space.

I made it through safe and sound without a scratch to my car! The driver right behind me could have done the same thing, but she hesitated. And just as she did, that gap suddenly closed up, trapping her vehicle in the pileup, and a spinning car slammed into her car.

So many times in the spiritual realm, we as Christians live too much on the defensive to the point of becoming totally passive. But you need to remember that *you* are the one who should be in control, not Satan. You have God-given authority in the Name of Jesus!

A person gets passive and timid spiritually when he allows the enemy to take control to some degree. What do I mean by that? Well, for example, in a sports competition, one team or another usually takes control of the game. One team usually sets the pace and dominates the game. And once that particular team gains control, they don't usually lose their momentum unless the other team rises up and takes back control of the game.

Spiritually speaking, you, not the devil, are supposed to be in control of your life! You're in the driver's seat, so to speak. You have the authority, and you are the one who should control a particular situation instead of allowing the situation to control *you*.

So stay in control! Keep your heel on the devil's head in your life and dance for joy because the victory is yours! Quit worrying and start believing!

We talked about not being ignorant of Satan's devices or wiles. The devil is deceitful. He uses devices or deceits to trick people into doubting God's Word and giving up on their faith. The devil tries to put fear on a child of God by masquerading himself as someone who has might and power over him.

But the devil has no might, power, or authority over the Christian unless the Christian lets him have authority — unless the Christian relinquishes or gives up his God-given authority! The devil only has authority over those in his kingdom. But the Christian has left that kingdom and has become a part of the Kingdom of God where God's Word is to rule and reign. And the Word says, "You are in control. You have power and authority in the Name of Jesus. Now what happens is up to you!"

The Apostle Peter says, ". . . *your adversary the devil, as a roaring lion, walketh about, seeking whom he MAY devour*" (1 Peter 5:8). Again, the Word is telling you that you are in control. The devil can only take control of you and devour you if you allow him to. So if you've been worrying, fretting, or having anxiety, quit allowing the devil to dominate you. Resist the devil and his thoughts! The Bible says that when you resist him, he *has* to flee (James 4:7).

You Have a Part To Play In Exercising Your Authority

First Peter 5:8 says the enemy is *as* a roaring lion, walking about, seeking whom he *may* devour. Now look at the preceding verse: *"Casting all your care upon him; for he careth for you"* (1 Peter 5:7).

Many people have the mistaken idea that casting their cares or burdens on the Lord means they are just to sit down and do nothing.

But you have a part to play in casting your cares on the Lord. You must find out what the Word says about how to live worry-free and then do something about it. Don't just sit there, despondent. *You* cast your cares upon the Lord!

You see, when God makes a promise, it is a contract between Him and His children. First Peter 5:7 is a contract between God and us. *He* has a responsibility, and *we* have a responsibility.

If you have children, you realize that you have certain responsibilities as parents, and your children have certain responsibilities. For example, after you teach your children certain things — the whats, hows, whens, wheres, and so forth — you expect them to do what you taught them.

Did you know that God expects something out of us as His children? He has given us instructions in His Word, and He expects something out of us. He tells us that He cares for us and that we are to give Him our cares, anxieties, and burdens. He promises that He will take them and work them all out. However, He also tells us not to pick those burdens back up again, but to go on down the road rejoicing and being busy doing the work of the Lord.

Psalm 55:22 says, *"Cast thy burden upon the Lord, and he shall sustain thee: he shall never suffer the righteous to be moved."* Notice here that before the Lord does His part, *you* have a specific part to play. In other words, before the Lord will sustain you, you have to cast your burdens on Him. Psalm 55:22 does *not* say, *"Carry* your burdens, and the Lord will sustain you."

If you want to carry your burdens, the Lord will let you. He will not *make* you cast your burdens on Him. He will not take them away from you against your will. But if you are willing to let go and trust Him, casting your worries and cares on Him, He will make a way of escape for you.

For example, in Acts 27, Paul was on board a ship headed for Rome, and the ship got caught in a storm. The ship was being torn apart, but Paul stood in the midst and said, *". . . be of good cheer: for there shall be no loss of any man's life among you, but of the ship. For there stood by me this night the angel of God, whose I*

am, and whom I serve" (Acts 27:22,23). God made a way
of escape for Paul. God even gave Paul the lives of those
who were with him on that ship: *". . . there shall be no
loss of any man's life among you. . . ."*

You, too, may be in the middle of a storm in your
life, but I want you to realize that you will not suffer
defeat if you cast your cares, your anxiety, and your
worry over on the Lord. He will sustain you and see you
through to victory!

Now an angel of the Lord may not stand by you and
tell you the outcome of your particular situation. But
One greater than an angel, the Lord Himself, said in
His Word to pray and not to worry or fear! *He* said, *"Be
careful* [anxious] *for nothing; but in every thing by
prayer and supplication with thanksgiving let your
requests be made known unto God"* (Phil. 4:6). He also
said, *"For God hath not given us the spirit of fear; but of
power, and of love, and of a sound mind"* (2 Tim. 1:7).

The Bible says, *"We have also a more SURE word of
prophecy . . ."* (2 Peter 1:19). This Word is greater than
an angel because the Word is God Himself speaking to
us. He gave us the *logos,* the written Word, so we could
believe it and speak out the *rhema,* the written Word
spoken, and live worry-free. We can live in joy and happiness as we cast our burdens and cares on the Lord.

We have authority over worry. God doesn't want us
burdened down with worry and the cares of life. You
remember we read First Peter 5:7: *"Casting all your care
upon him; for he careth for you."* God cares about us!

Some people get in the position of feeling that God doesn't care about them. But most of the time, those feelings are brought on by bad decisions they've made in life. Maybe they made a certain decision, and when things didn't go their way, they began to feel sad, dejected, and unloved. Then they began to feel that even God didn't care. They may have even blamed Him that things turned out the way they did.

But it's in those times that we need to look to God and run *to* Him, not *away* from Him.

God does care! He cares for you now, and He will always care. And if you will stay true to Him even in the midst of the storm and keep your heart right before Him, He will bring you out!

Your Victory Depends on You!

Sometimes we make the mistake of blaming others around us — our friends, family, business associates, and so forth — for our problems. But too many times, *we* — the person we saw when we looked in the mirror this morning — are our own problem!

Some people just don't like to take responsibility for themselves. They like to pass the responsibility off on somebody else, and they like to pass the blame to somebody else when things go wrong. Children often do that. For example, a child will say, "Well, if it hadn't been for Little Brother, that never would have happened."

Sometimes adults try to lay the blame for something on God. They'll say, "Well, God didn't do what He said He was going to do."

Well, if God didn't do something for someone that He said He was going to do, it's because that person didn't do what God told *him* to do!

God cares about each and every one of us the same. He will not fail to come through for anyone who puts his trust in Him. He will sustain him. He will not let the righteous fall!

Psalm 55:22 says, "... *he shall never suffer the righteous to be moved* [or fall]."

Notice it *didn't* say, "He shall never suffer those who *claim* to be righteous to be moved." It didn't say, "... those who run with the righteous crowd ..." or "... those who are hanging out at church on Sundays...."

No, it says, "... those who are *righteous.* ..." In other words, it's talking about those who are doers of the Word — those who obey God and His Word.

It's also talking about those who are willing to accept responsibility for themselves and who will do something for themselves instead of just sitting around, waiting to blame someone else for their failures.

You see, you can't ride on the corporate faith of your church congregation in your own personal walk with God. You can't ride on someone else's coattail. It's not coattail faith; it's a personal, living relationship between God and *you.* God cares for *you*! And *you* have to cast your cares on Him to receive His blessings and benefits in your life.

Many people "cop out" of their responsibility for their own life by saying, "Well, my church doesn't believe that, so I can't be responsible for obeying it."

But what do *you* believe? If you want to be blessed in life, you have to have enough backbone to stand up and take responsibility to obey God for yourself. If you will take a stand on what you believe, you will find that God will give you the strength to stand. He cares!

Sometimes it seems that it's easier just to drag along down in the dumps and feel sorry for yourself than it is to do something about your situation. But God requires something of you.

Remember Psalm 55:22 says, *"Cast thy burden upon the Lord, and he shall sustain thee: he shall never suffer the righteous to be moved."* You see, this verse says God will sustain you, but it also says *you* have to do something: *You* have to cast your burden on the Lord!

You may have to do something to get yourself out of the "mulligrubs." You may have to give yourself a pep talk or encourage yourself in the Lord (*see* 1 Sam. 30:6). But just knowing that God cares is a great comfort and encouragement.

You may have missed it and sinned in some area, so you think God doesn't care about you anymore. But no matter what you've done or haven't done that's wrong, God still cares. However, it's up to you whether or not you go to Him for help. What happens in your particular situation depends on you.

God has given you authority, but He's not going to do something in your life without your cooperation.

For example, someone who has a problem with smoking cigarettes or using bad language can trust God to help and deliver him. But God is probably not going to just deliver that person on His own without some cooperation from the person. In other words, that person at least has to admit he has a problem, and he has to decide he wants to be delivered.

People often say, "God, take this habit away from me!" But many times, they say that because they don't want to take any responsibility or make any effort themselves. God will help them get rid of the habit, but He won't just take it away without any cooperation on their part.

You see, *you're* going to have to do something about your situation. For example, First Peter 5:7 says, *"Casting all your care upon him; for he careth for you."* So, first, you're going to have to actively cast your cares upon the Lord.

You might also have to do something about your situation in the natural. For example, some people who make wrong decisions and get into trouble financially will pray, "Oh, God, help me out of this situation!" But then they don't do anything themselves.

God will meet you where you are, but you have to work with Him. For example, if you're behind in paying your bills, you may have to work two jobs for a while. You may have to cut back on your spending. But no matter what you have to do, you still need to trust God and cast your cares upon Him. He cares for you!

Now if you're facing financial difficulties, what I'm telling you to do may not be any fun, but it is one way to get out of the circumstances you're facing. You may have to put in more hours working than you really want to. But just realize that God cares for you and that He will work with you if you'll work with Him.

God says, "I will bless what you put your hand to" (Ps. 1:3). So you can't just sit down and say, "Lord, I'm just living by faith. Help me, Lord; do something for me. Bless me now" and then expect to receive something. No, you have to act in line with His Word. You have to get up and do something.

For example, if I didn't have a job, I'd cast the care and the burden of that situation over on the Lord. But then I wouldn't stay in bed until 12:00 noon! I'd get up and go out into the workforce where they're hiring people. They're not hiring people in my bedroom! They're not hiring people in my living room or den where I'm reading or watching the news!

You see, it's one thing to say, "Well, praise the Lord. I believe God." It's another thing to put some "feet" to your faith!

> **JAMES 2:18,20**
> **18 Yea, a man may say, Thou hast faith, and I have works: shew me thy faith without thy works, and I will shew thee my faith by my works. . . .**
> **20 But wilt thou know, O vain man, that faith without works is dead?**

James is telling us here that it doesn't matter how much you believe God, you have to show your faith by your works.

Some people don't like to read that part of James because it has to do with work! It has to do with getting up and doing something. It has to do with them personally taking some responsibility to believe God and then acting on what they believe.

We have God-given authority to rule and reign in life over worry, fear, or any adverse situation or circumstance that may come our way. But we have to learn how to use that authority and start walking free from those things that try to put us in bondage.

Maybe you've been bound with worry and fear, and you need to take action according to the Word so you can put yourself in position to receive victory. You may need to change what you've been doing and start rolling your cares over on the Lord and casting down thoughts that are contrary to His Word.

Or perhaps you know *how* to live worry-free, but you may need to take an inventory of your life. Peter talked about stirring up the people's pure minds by way of remembrance (2 Peter 3:1).

In other words, we all need to be reminded of these truths from time to time. We need to take an inventory of our lives to make sure we are living worry-free the way God wants us to live.

Rise Up and Use Your Authority in Christ!

Some people just "rock along" at times, not bothering to check up on themselves to see if they've given any place to the devil in their minds. Everything seems to be going fine in their lives. But then one day, the devil attacks and knocks them sideways! Before they know it, they're worrying, fretting, and having anxiety. Why? Because they haven't been casting their cares on the Lord. They've been allowing the enemy to come in and begin taking control of their mind.

But I tell you what. If you'll continually check up on yourself to make sure the devil doesn't try to put even the least little bit of worry in your mind, then he can't have any place in you to try to defeat you.

You need to take your responsibility to cast down any thought that is contrary to God's Word, whether it be worry, fear, unforgiveness, and so forth. For example, you may see someone on the street who's wronged you, and a thought may come to your mind, *Don't speak to him. Remember what he did to you?*

In that case, your response should be, "Yes, Mr. Devil, I am going to speak to him. In fact, if you don't shut up, I'm going to give him a five-dollar gift!"

The devil needs to know you mean business with him and that you're serious about the Word of God. If you aren't, the devil will keep coming back to try to hound you. In the middle of the night, he'll wake you up with thoughts such as, *"What are you going to do about such-and-such? What if such-and-such happens?*

You have to stay on top of those thoughts all the time and cast them down with the Word of God. The devil is not a gentleman!

Now the Holy Spirit *is* a Gentleman. He will work on your behalf when you ask Him to. He will only come into your situation and help you if you open the door and allow Him to. But the devil will kick down the door if you give him place. He will kick the door down and run right over the top of it into your life whether you want him there or not!

The devil doesn't have any authority over you if you're walking in line with the Word — if you're not giving place to him through thoughts, words, and actions that are contrary to the Word. The Bible says you have the authority to reign in life by Christ Jesus (Rom. 5:17). But to do it, you're going to have to keep the Word of God in your heart, in your mind, and in your mouth.

Then when the devil tries to kick the door down in your life by putting thoughts in your mind, *you* start using the sword of the Spirit — the Word of God — on him! I like to think that in a sense you are saying, "Holy Ghost, get him!"

I once heard a funny story about a fellow who broke into a certain house to rob it. There was a parrot in the house, and the parrot kept saying to the fellow, "The devil's going to get you. The devil's going to get you."

The parrot kept saying that over and over again. Suddenly, the man heard something behind him. He turned around and saw a big Doberman Pinscher, snarling and growling and showing his fangs.

The parrot then said, "I told you he's going to get you!"

I don't know if that dog's name was "the devil" or not, but I think you can see the point. It's a funny story, and you may laugh at it. But in your own life, you need to tell the devil, "The Holy Ghost is going to get you! If you mess with me, the Holy Ghost is going to get you!"

You see, the devil is a defeated foe, and we are victorious in Christ. So let's use our authority and not give the devil any place in our lives.

Pray this prayer out loud: "Thank you, Father, for helping me to do what Your Word says to do and to go forth and receive what is mine — what belongs to me in Christ. Lord, I'm giving my worries and cares to You. I'm not going to carry those burdens anymore. I'm going to walk by faith, trusting You. I'm going to see the victory with the eye of faith and use my authority in Christ over worry. Thank You for the answer. It's done! In Jesus' Name, amen."

No matter how big or small the tests and trials of life are that may surround you, you also have a loving God who is surrounding you with His care! He is bigger than any test, trial, situation, or circumstance that may come your way to defeat you, and He will see you through to victory. So cast all your cares on the Lord once and for all, and begin living your life worry-free!